Love Born Out Of Chao

Love Poet

Written and edited by
Delawrence Jones

Printed by Amazon.com, Inc

ISBN: 9781718116863

Table Of Contents

A Sound In The Silence

In the silence of the night

I hear the echo of my own thoughts;

Waiting to be spoken to any ear that is brought.

Tell me if you're familiar,

With this sound...

In the silence of the night

I become the things I've been running from;

All of the bad suffocating the good until there is none.

Tell me if you've ever heard this sound, just once.

In the silence of the night

My heartbeat is a melody I can live with.

I hear the history of my pain and joy in the rhythm of it.

I know this sound must be somewhat familiar..

In the silence of the night,

My doubts disappear and the truth draws near.

I can drown the world in a single tear,

But right now, that is not the sound I hear.

This is the sound of being alone that I used to fear..

She Is Poetry

Beautiful women never impressed me.

But beautiful women with good intentions

Arrest me.

They bind my soul into wedlock.

Her eyes scream "don't forget me"

Yet her presence is never gifted freely.

It always comes at a cost.

She tells me time is more valuable than money;

So I can't help but wonder "What's her price?"

She could tell me "forever" and Id find the time.

She reminds me why diamonds shine;

That pressure brings your beauty to the surface..

Sometimes she wants more for me than I do.

She says "step outside of your comfort zone and into the light"..

And I'm still afraid to leave this prison that is my mind..

Where she exists for all time, without time.

I tell her it's deeper than love.

Its destiny.

Something already foretold in our God's diary.

We are his greatest secrets

And she is the most beautiful whisper on the wind, called "poetry".

To My Loved Ones

If you died before telling your story,

I promise to tell it for you.

I'll convey your energy,

but your secrets are still safe with me.

I can be your diary.

Write your past in my memories

And I'll never forget.

Hearts cast deception in many directions

But hearts in casts may dim your perception.

Maybe you should heal.

I'll be right here for the whole thing.

I can't wait to see who you become

And what your blessings bring.

If money is your motive,

Don't lose sight of what the real goal is.

Take care of your loved ones and take care when you love One.

We've all been victims and villains at a time;

So understand that I understand you.

Even if our goals don't align, your wishes are mine.

So I'll pray over your life, as if that too, were mine.

Acts

People tend to fall for acts,

Meanwhile I fall for acts of kindness.

I understand the ego,

And how it's our cause for blindness.

Heavy emotions keep us mindless.

Especially those dark ones;

The ones most hard to hide under the sun.

It's so much easier to trust someone's actions and patterns,

Than try to guess what they're thinking or feeling.

Acts of kindness light us up like Jack O Lanterns,

As we try to show love to those worth healing.

Sometimes I wonder if some people are worth dealing with,

But then I remember; I'm the one worth being with.

Come and talk to me, genuinely.

Most people act like who they wish to be.

But when we exchange words, feelings and minds;

You'll see, I prefer to come as I am.

Bird's Eye

I'm

Self conscious in a self-righteous world.

My character is of the bounce in my curl.

I wanna be a black bird

Against the night sky.

As free as my third eye.

From my perspective,

It is clear where the truth lies.

Somewhere in your eyes,

Where beauty is recognized...

Don't get lost in the moment,

Momentarily own it.

I'm reaping the future before I've sewn it.

You call it perception

But I perceive an extra component.

I am not a philosopher, I am just the exponent.

I swear that I've seen it all.

The ugly and the beautiful.

The Real Hue

How many times do we have to die

To realize life is never ending?

That limits are temporary; even the sky,

And rules are worth bending.

We should be breaking bold boundaries,

Become infatuated with spiritual Intel,

Shaking your nervous shivers; the present is not so scary.

Do whatever brings you joy,

Because there's no telling we'll ever make it to hell.

Learn to find beauty in everything ugly

Because everything has a story.

I guarantee you fall in love

With everything around you.

The colors will be more vibrant,

And you'll recognize the real hue..

<u>What Is Love?</u>

What is Love?

It's not that I've never known

It's just never been clear;

I mean, it's not that I've never owned,

It's just never been here.

I guess we've all stolen hearts,

We've all seen how easily they fall apart.

What Is Love?

I guess I could have went searching,

But then I'd have never found Me.

These are the feelings that make you drown deep,

Like you're gasping for air from your sound sleep.

What is Love?

And how does it define us?

When we receive it, oh how it refines us

Because for too long we've been giving and giving up.

What is Love?

Other than your beautiful perception.

What is Love?

I suppose it's what we strive to be.

I bet Love has everything to do with the way we see.

Take a look, and you know it's me.

I'd roam in search of your heart, like my own Odyssey.

I know love has to be more than the search for perfection.

It has something to do with compassion.

It is something you can not ration.

If you give it, give it all and never regret it.

And know it might not be reciprocated, so never expect it.

We are like the lights we see in the sky

Trying to distinguish the ways we shine, you and I.

Because we set each other's hearts on fire...

Hate cannot extinguish us.

So, what is Love?

It's everything and it's nothing.

It's what you're missing when you're forgetting "something".

It's the only thing that fills the void,

It's what makes a man, of a boy.

I am Love.

Paper Soldier

These emotions I engrave on paper

Helped me find myself.

Who would've thought that they'd become vapor

And clear the path to inner wealth.

I'm speaking of mental health.

I bet invisibility wouldn't be enough stealth

To avoid the things I've felt.

Oh, these emotions.

I run away with them.

From plotting passion with pen point precision,

To wallowing in the inception of depression..

Before I ever see it, I feel the vision.

I guess they call it empathy.

And the path to these emotions

Was not easy.

We all know life is dirty, greasy;

Wish I could wipe my hands with the stuff,

But that's the same as giving up;

And there's just too much I'd be giving up...

Look N' Show

These days it's hard to tell what you're thinking.

You leave me in the dark like a starless evening.

I'm searching in your eyes for a light to kindle sparks.

I would give up my pride for a seat just rows a part

From you...

Open your mind to me,

I am not the enemy;

And if that's clear to see

Then show me there is more to what could be...

She Knows

She knows

If she says "I Love You",

It just might be too soon.

She can't sleep at night

So she rises with the moon.

Hoping someday their hearts beat in tune.

Give her love some room.

I mean, her love's a womb

Giving birth to aspirations in men.

She knows

She's a muse,

That only a fool would lose.

Be careful with her heart,

Because she'll never be the same

After it's broken or bruised.

She knows.

She can build the perfect man

With the proper tools.

She spins his thoughts and dreams,

Like yarn from wool.

And he knows that she knows these things.

But still, it is so hard to please a Queen.

I mean, what does he know?

To Love In Vain

We paint on the walls of each other hearts,

All of our hopes and dreams.

But as soon as what we were building falls apart,

We lose these things.

Every time, you lose a piece of yourself.

Then you self reflect to collect on that intellect.

We used to argue about the dumbest things.

It always turned out to be a misunderstanding.

No matter how long our love fell and failed,

I would keep standing.

But in your eyes I felt the distance.

And you would never grant me admittance.

Just false affirmations that your love is still mine.

We're not the same as we started out

But that's not really the problem.

I sense that we lost the motivation

To keep learning about our love and who we place it in.

And maybe all this work on yourself

Calls for a vacation.

You take your time but I won't be waitin'.

I'll rest when I'm assured;

So rest assured I'll always want to be yours.

Poetry In My Veins

Poetry all in my veins,

If you slit them, they would riddle.

Played my thoughts like a fiddle,

Off my tongue they would sizzle.

Taste my food for thought for progression.

Await my mind, distraught and lost,

Yet still in my possession.

On my soul, I write straight from the soul-ar plexus.

I wish that I could free us all from the vices that vex us.

Sentimental on my mental,

If I loved, I never meant to.

Who's to say what's right for you,

Plotting on a life for two

That multiplies, alright that's cool.

But since I write my own story

We're gone make it HIS-story.

I'm just in the making,

And Like words on paper, I just can't weight..

Who's to blame this pain that I just can't take

Writing words all day,

That's just how I play.

And if I make it on the way,

Then it was meant to be.

I've got poetry in my veins.

A Heart Called, "Home"

It was clear to me right away

That you didn't feel the same way.

But I let people get in my head,

And tell me this is how the game's played.

Would love to be in Love,

But sometimes it feels like no escape.

I know the danger of feelings that don't reciprocate.

And just because my feelings are deeper than yours,

Doesn't equate to hate.

You know what they say about jealousy,

And as much I try to avoid it,

My heart is too filled with love,

Not to deploy it.

I just want you to bask in it;

But if you've already made up your mind,

I guess there's no point in askin' it.

I just hope you find Love,

Even if it isn't mine.

I'm walking a thin line between isolation

And loneliness.

I Used to get lost in your eyes, but now I remember where home is.

No one can convince me that being alone equates to loneliness.

Things are safer like this.

I Am Convinced

It was clear to me right away

That you didn't feel the same way.

But I let people get in my head,

And tell me this is how the game's played.

Would love to be in Love,

But sometimes it feels like no escape.

I know the danger of feelings that don't reciprocate.

And just because my feelings are deeper than yours,

Doesn't equate to hate.

You know what they say about jealousy,

And as much I try to avoid it,

My heart is too filled with love,

Not to deploy it.

I just want you to bask in it;

But if you've already made up your mind,

I guess there's no point in askin' it.

I just hope you find Love,

Even if it isn't mine.

I'm walking a thin line between isolation

And loneliness.

I Used to get lost in your eyes, but now I remember where home is.

No one can convince me that being alone equates to loneliness.

Things are safer like this.

Distraught

As this world falls apart,

I taste the tears of angels in the rain.

I ponder thoughts that never reach outside the windowpane..

This is my pain.

Isolated by their opinions,

So I made my mind and soul my dominion...

But it's hard to hold hate for a soul,

When I know we're all

sinnin'.

So pray with me.

That our demons never prosper.

Quit acting like a fool,

for the soul receives no Oscar.

I'm sorry momma.

If all the prayers that I sent for you

Never get a answered.

Then I'm the cause for the cancer.

I mean, maybe this is my karma.

I don't mean to alarm ya',

But I often stress over the next comma.

This that soul talk as I reflect on my old faults.

I've got skeletons in my closet, demons in my vault.

It's hard to open up to people and tell them why I'm so distraught.

I've been lied to more than the average so I hardly trust a lot...

A Good Thing

I've been focused on too many of the wrong things lately.

I hope there is still enough time to save me.

I'm learning to count my blessings,

Sometimes more than once.

And I'm thanking God for every experience,

Even the bad ones.

If I just could see the world through his eyes,

Or figure out how we've strayed so far...

If I could just sit with Adam and Eve and exchange thoughts.

Tell them about all of the suffering they've brought.

Just imagine the information Id receive;

The clarity that Id achieve...

The Good Book often seems to good to be true,

But that's the beauty in it.

It's the one good thing, that never goes bad.

It's Only Love

A man is just a man until a woman loves him.

Put your hands inside of mine,

And then put your life in them.

She counts the stars in his eyes,

Unaware she placed them there.

Her love in the dark is just like a flare.

Only a woman knows how to pick a man a part.

She tells him let his heart be a secret,

Not a shopping cart.

How can we afford to be allured by so many detours?

I know we have all felt it before,

The uncertainty that eats at our core..

Even when we're satisfied, it never lasts

So we search for more..

A woman's only a woman until she meets her best friend.

A Man, who kisses her forehead and fingertips;

Makes love to her undiscovered mind.

When she's alone she rewinds

Moments.

But When he's alone, she runs through his mind

And never goes home.

Because home is where the heart is.

He paints emotions like an artist.

Heaven's daughters are his muse.

He tries to heal them from broken hearts and abuse.

But he hardly ever gets the chance.

Because his fantasy is romance,

And his reality is the opposite at second glance.

He's aware she has so many men she could run to,

And Love is only Love when there's two..

So, he gives up on you..

Die For You

I used to think that Love was my mission.

But now it's obvious that it's just a bonus.

Either way,

Ain't no way I could fail.

I tell myself, that's the old us.

You know,

Just because we're men,

Doesn't mean we don't feel safe when you hold us.

How can we ever shine in your eyes

If you never behold us?

Like shooting stars, we travel far and wide..

Just to feel the pull of these strings we tied.

If it was no strings attached maybe we'd let go someday.

But I can't help but feel like dying for your love today.

<u>Growing Up</u>

As a child

The world was a lot more simple.

A galaxy existed in someone's eyes

And my favorite compliment was about my dimples.

As a teenager

I learned how complex we could be.

How Love is the true gateway drug,

And heartbreak is an overdose of apathy.

As a teen I found out

That wherever you watered,

The grass would be green;

That its worthwhile to invest in the unseen.

As an adult I figured out

That 90% of what I already knew

Was worthless.

I'm still learning to fight programmed urges.

Like, asking my mom's consent before making a purchase

As a kid they never told us that

Aging would feel this good and bad.

I mean, I always knew you couldn't get lost time back,

But what I wouldn't give to go back.

When You Look At Me

I am not the most sociable

Nor approachable.

Or so I've been told.

I guess I hardly notice because

I'm so busy noticing others.

So busy being amazed at their existence.

I'm not captivated by the similarities,

I fall in love with the difference.

Of course,

You can't tell everyone their special.

The ego is the devil's playground;

Where mood swings send logic airborne.

We are all undeniably unique.

From our head to our feet.

I just wonder what you see,

When you look at me.

Look, Love

Look, Love.

It's too hot the way our passion burns.

Look, Love.

I know you love the way our hearts learn

From pain.

I'd never hurt it,

Or watch it break again.

Would you take a look, Love?

I can't find you in the air.

But I found love in a broken woman

Barely coping but hoping for genuine Lovin'.

I can't call it; and I can't call you.

You put me on Cloud 9,

And then I fall through; fall for you.

I barely have the patience,

Awaiting your touch and fragrance.

It's The sweetest, wish I could save it.

Give me a placement...

Somewhere deep in your heart,

And I'll call it home.

Look, Love..

This is how you feel.

A Subliminal Feeling

I

Treasure you deeply.

Like ocean blues that never end,

I sing for you.

Women become bereaved who seek me.

Because I tell them I can't stay, their love won't do.

You can't change my heart.

It shops for love like an open cart,

But once I find my item we'll never depart.

You. ARE. Beauty.

Beheld by me, but the world is not blind either.

You leave me speechless like I need a breather.

We could shake this joint like a seizure

And smoke joints by the waves.

With enough money for anytime to be leisure.

Some gentlemen love a certain way,

We never learned to behave.

I'm reckless with this.

I'd overdose on a single kiss,

Like the drug was your lips..

<u>9-5</u>

How many times

Will I sell my soul

For a 9-5?

Death to my dreams

But at least

The weekends are "Live".

Look at all the hours gone

From 9 to 5.

From the morning to the night;

Can I really say I've lived?

Its suicide to kill yourself for a livin';

Then to visit death in the dreams that we're given.

It's a cycle of crucifixion.

We only pray because we're sinnin'.

And there's really no stoppin',

It's not even an option.

We feel alive in the moonlight

Because we were dying for that moment.

Just to feel the relief and release.

I sort of feel like that's when the devil is at his peak.

Awaiting to reap the souls of the meek.

I Boycott the parties and the Streets

Because I see that its a set up.

We sell our souls all day

And at night the devil collects.

It only seems sinister in retrospect;

I'm on the outside looking in

Where I can warn you before its your turn.

Saving lives and saving souls

Is only a few words away

So again I say

How many times

will we sell our souls

For a 9-5..?

Don't Be Afraid

You don't deserve an undercover Love.

You deserve the type that's bright as light.

I often overstep my boundaries,

But I tread light.

Don't underestimate your potential,

Turn your dreams into a vivid visual.

Watch as someday the Impossible becomes plausible.

We are greater than our flaws, you know?

I hope these efforts echo

In your mind.

Don't be afraid to show

That it's more to you than just a beautiful face.

You tackle issues with grace.

Don't be afraid to cry, just dry your face.

And keep your eyes on the prize until one win multiplies.

In the sky we'll be immortalized.

So, for now just keep an open heart and open mind.

And never be afraid to die,

Because we never really die.

I think I read that in a book and it left my soul shook;

To think about the memories plagiarized and took..

The Heart

I bet it's hard to be you

But it's hard to be me too.

There is beauty in our struggles

And healing in our pain.

You can call me on the double

When your tears mimic rain.

There's a drought in my heart,

I'll probably never love again.

Take these broken pieces,

But be careful 'cuz their sharp.

Every time we get played,

Hearts cry like a harp.

It's like music to the villain's ears.

Seek no remorse from a hollow corpse.

Life is hard, so I peek at yours.

Wonder if we feel the same.

Or am I just going insane.

I'm so caught up in the little things,

The bigger picture is belittling.

Thumbs forever fiddling

With hearts that have lost rhythm.

The heart and mind battle schisms,

It's a war for dominance.

Ode to lovely memories

That pray we don't forget 'em.

Hearts build walls like layered denim.

I call but an echo answers.

We fall for love and never return

We forget that we're birds

Held down by the things we've learned

And the things that we yearn.

They say love is in the air,

But only so high 'til it burns.

I say that love is in our hearts,

And evil's at every turn.

So, whatever it is we're looking for

We'll probably never find.

When She Says, "I Love You"

Every time she says "I Love You"

It saves my soul a little;

From the deepest, darkest depths

Of myself.

Where my demons lurk

And put me through hell.

I've collected the pieces of hearts so brittle.

We've all been played before.

But when we're both to blame,

Who's the musician and who's the fiddle?

And when she says "I Love You"

I almost believe it.

Her voice is so convincing,

But when I observe her actions

I don't perceive it.

I'm no saint,

I'm sure she feels the same.

I bet she wonders

"How can this nigga lie to my face?

He tries to cheat me like some cheap game

And when i return the favor,

The bitter-sweet taste is hard to savor."

We're no good for one another,

But the sex makes us think otherwise.

And the only thing I hated more than other guys

Was the number of lies.

Why tell me you're looking for love,

When you clearly desire lust?

Why do we say "I love you"

And then jeopardize "Us"?..

And then I realized..

That because whenever you say it,

I want it to be true,

So then I feel it too.

Knowing deep down,

Im probably not the one for you..

Oh,

Don't cut yourself on this heart;

Fragile as paper.

Instead write your worries on my lines-

Here your secrets are safer..

Where love lives, because love saves lives;

Even though our short Forever

Was destroyed by lies.

Soul Talk

There are songs

That I hate.

Because they make me

Think of you.

I know that

The time is late

For confessions.

But

You used to make me

Forget the blues.

You're an array of

Vibrant colors.

I can feel the light.

I find it hard

To apologize

Because I know

I'm "sorry" in your eyes.

I'm just another loser

Too bruised to

Accept the truth

Nor exploit the lies.

Shit,

You make it easy

To cry.

Don't tell my mother,

Can't let her know

I hurt inside.

Rather lay on

Your breast

And speak to

Your soul

For a while.

She Is Poetry

Beautiful women never impressed me.

But beautiful women with good intentions

Arrest me.

They bind my soul into wedlock.

Her eyes scream "don't forget me"

Yet her presence is never gifted freely.

It always comes at a cost.

She tells me time is more valuable than money;

So I can't help but wonder "What's her price?"

She could tell me "forever" and Id find the time.

She reminds me why diamonds shine;

That pressure brings your beauty to the surface..

Sometimes she wants more for me than I do.

She says "step outside of your comfort zone and into the light"..

And i'm still afraid to leave this prison that is my mind..

Where she exists for all time, without time.

I tell her it's deeper than love.

Its destiny.

Something already foretold in our God's diary.

We are his greatest secrets

And she is the most beautiful whisper on the wind, called "poetry".

10:15PM Confessions

I get tongue tied when I try to

Evade temptations.

Forgive me for the women I've lied to;

They just weren't you.

Tell me if it's too late to admit

That a connection is due.

Are you too far gone

In someone else's Love

To see me anymore?..

Missed chances

And second guessed thoughts.

This is how my doom is to be brought.

Maybe I should have told you

"I love you"

Sooner, rather than later.

But now there's another man you cater

And the taste is too bitter to savor.

I'm a lost cause

Without the effect you have

On me..

<u>Timeline</u>

They say don't live in the past

But those tend to be the best days.

I could tell you how it felt

To fall in love on my birthday.

I know these things never progress us,

But neither does the future caress us.

No promised days known to man.

I hope someday we save this land

And peace is how we take a stand.

Sometimes I feel like,

The future is just as mine as the past is.

I see the signs between the lines

Without glasses..

Or maybe I'm dreaming..

True words from the mind

Of someone just like you.

Stuck in time,

Lending you a line

Of rhythm to run on..

Rest Easy

Lay your head

On my chest.

You'll breathe better, Love.

You're a dream

Worth remembering.

You give me

A vibe worth centering.

It's hard to let go.

Your pain can be felt for forever.

You're an open book of love letters.

Sure, you have your walls

Yet,

Your heart creates connections

That won't sever.

So, rest your eyes.

Know that the future

See's you coming, too.

Don't be surprised

When the days and nights

Pray for you.

And I hope they make a way for two

So that we don't have to

Close our eyes

And forget one another..

Sun Day

Lately I've been caught up

Within my own depth

And I need help to be brought up.

I'm forever lost in my thoughts

Trying to daydream a new reality.

Whatever it may cost,

I just need change drastically.

I hold out my empty cup.

Do you have anything to offer?

I pray as the times get harder,

My heart only gets softer.

I'm bitter from many losses.

I'm tired of being cautious.

I'm nauseous from these mirages.

I'm seeing things in my distant future..

Or maybe it's just the Sun playing tricks on me.

I wonder if the Son ever prays for me..

Because I feel alone on this journey.

It's hard to admit when its hurting,

But its hurts less

With these lessons I'm learning.

I'm aware that I'm being molded.

Messages so deeply coded

In my dreams

And the people closest.

To be a part of the bigger scheme;

I hardly think they chose it.

Seize the mind and keep it open.

Fight for your dreams, because you're chosen.

Everything under the Son/Sun ain't golden;

There's a lot of light that we hold in.

So, know that the darkness we see

Is just another illusion.

<u>A Timely Love</u>

I'd rather not really know

Where we're all supposed to go,

Because Love is the only road.

Whether it is rain or snow,

I know that we will find a path;

I prefer the overcast.

Seek a mind as deep as

A Love that will forever last.

I know its

Easier said than done

When you're living by an hourglass;

Time is slipping too fast.

I think that I would rather know,

How much time is left to go

Before I meet the end of the road..

Light Work

To myself

I give all the trust.

Shining like diamond dust.

I am peeking through the crust

Of the new me.

Made in the image

Of the One;

So what if gods do bleed.

I mean,

I'm barely a blemish of the Source.

He's the key to Life

That opens doors.

Providing signs that steer your course.

So, we don't remain loss,

Unless by choice.

Just give me the light

And I will show you

The way.

Barriers, with time, fall.

I am just a night call

Away.

If you need advice,

I'm here to stay.

Just don't blow me off

Or blow me away

Like your favorite flowers.

I Just Want You

I just want you.

More than anything

That this world can give me.

I've run it through my mind

A thousand times.

Trying to picture the perfect

Moments.

But it's never as real as

You being right next to me.

Love

Don't make me too blind to see.

Show me your flaws

And your philosophies.

I can't fall in Love

Because I'm constantly asking

"Are We There Yet?".

Are we THERE yet?..

I just want you.

More than anything

I've ever wanted.

But I know that

You don't always get

What you want.

So, I'm still..

Falling.

<u>Love Lecture</u>

Words sliding off your tongue

Really bring me alive.

Would you walk into my life?

Or,

Would you run to a lie?

We have

Been skin to skin,

Laced in sin;

It's already too late.

You can't run from feelings

Because your heart

Is in Love with the race.

Can't be living for the chase

of a heart

That's only destined

To break

You know the devil

Plays his part

In trying to

Keep us away...

Probably what I'd say

If I was in Love.

Words like liquid Lust,

In a bedroom;

It's' only us..

Fall in love with a Queen

She'll turn a man

Into a Prince.

Let her touch

Work magic

On your soul,

Young Warrior.

Come close

And catch a case

Of this

Addicting Euphoria.

Butterflies in your stomach

Wouldn't make you

A Mad Man..

The birds and the bees

Taught me

Young.

Love is life,

And until its

Unconditional,

You've only begun..

Don't Forget To Mention

Oh,

You make it hard

To stay patient.

I think of all

The hours I've been waiting;

It's the feel of angst I'm hating.

It's not you.

Well it is.

Because I hate the way

You got control of me.

You're leading me down

A path I would rather do without.

If I go with the flow

I'm afraid I might drown.

But it would be worth it

Just to taste your waters.

I'll die and be reborn in my perfect form.

You're like a song that I adorn,

Plus its sexy when you scorn

Me.

We could lie

Here on this floor

Begging each other for more.

Or drench the bed

In liquid passion,

Releasing our tensions.

Pay attention.

My time isn't cheap.

My loving is up

For honorable mention.

So, don't forget to mention..

Beast, In The Belly Of

I have a bad habit of confessing my heart and my secrets.

Don't bother trying to save my dignity;

Just leave it.

Now, I could tell you who I'm bleeding for,

And left me with this leaking core

But I don't even know anymore.

There's been too many occasions,

And way too much frustration.

I feel like,

If Beyonce was better at Fighting Temptations,

She would have never fell in love with a heathen.

That is quite the familiar sensation,

And repetitive correlation

To my own life.

Because the truth hits hard

And makes it tough to breathe in.

I'm at war in the belly of the beast

Whom is swimming in the deep end.

So even if I escape,

There's another monster to face.

Whether its my reflection in the water

Or my soul at the altar..

Attraction

I'm so attracted to you.

Everything that you do,

It drives me crazy.

One plus one equals two,

But I feel one with you.

I don't need my math checked.

All I care is about the sum of us.

How will we end up?

Will I adore you for a day?

Only for you to just fade away?

Lord knows I can't afford another delay,

Because I crave your touch.

Shit,

But how would we end up?

Will our

Eager "Good Morning"'s

Soon turn to dry "Sup"'s?

I've lived this cycle many times.

So, I need certainty.

I need to hear that you'll love me.

Not today, but someday.

Yeah, I tend to get ahead of myself.

But I'm just so attracted to you.

So infatuated

That it's becoming complicated.

Every minute wasted

Is a moment being hated

By me.

I'd rather you be close enough

To taste the words

85

That I've barely begun to speak.

So close,

That eye contact leaves us weak

With butterflies...

I'm attracted to you

In a way that I can't describe.

I long to know

How you feel inside.

When you're

Sad

Happy

Angry;

I want to be there for it all.

But every time I get my hopes up,

I wonder if it's all for nothing.

You see,

I've never seen Forever in person.

So, it leads me to believe

That all attraction is fleeting and deceitful.

We never get what we really seek in the end.

And that is that who we desire

Can live up to our dreams

And the fictions we've written in our hearts.

So,

As much as I adore you,

And pray that we would be everything

That we could be;

How would we end up?

What would be the sum of my dreams and yours?..

Madly In Love

She loved the idea

Of love...

A love as deep as

The depths of the eyes

Of her lover.

But they just couldn't

Seem to get each other.

She was a lonely, blank page

In a never ending love story..

She'd drown in her own rage,

Madly in love with this man's glory.

Dying to get close..

Harsh Words, Soft Tongue

I've committed murder

With words as sweet and soft

As cotton candy..

Yes,

You receive the words

Readily and Easily

Because that is my intention,

But the truth will still burn you

Before setting you free,

My friend.

Is this not a sign

Of my love for you?

<u>My Materials</u>

I lack the accomplishments

And possessions

That most women

Search for in a man.

But I possess all

Of the intangibles

She craves to feel

Without her hands.

..Who will love me?

The Gateway Drug

Poetry is a gateway drug

To feeling everything.

It is the product of thoughts

That lack a voice

To be heard.

It lives in all of us.

<u>Enough</u>

I tend to say

Too much

When I am tired

Of not saying

ENOUGH.

Rain, Rain

She was like the rain

Falling for me without fail.

I tried to hold her

In my hands,

But she could not be kept.

Rain, Rain.

Don't go away.

<u>Just Do It</u>

Have you ever met an Early Bird?

Wings barely stretched,

Struggling to embrace the day;

But he knows

There is work to be done

If he wants to eat.

Have you ever met the Worm?

Moist with slime and dew,

Inching along its way.

Aware that a prayer

Won't save him from being prey;

And yet still

He ventures into the Great Unknown.

L.I.A.R., L.I.A.R.

Lies never get very far because

karma is too Inclined

to keep justice Alive

speak and Reply with truth,

and blessings will arrive.

you risk becoming a Little

too Infamous,

all the while, spreading Apathy;

with every untruth your tongue Rises.

Instead

Give birth to a new world

With every truthful word.

Marooned Lover

I am writing to you to say

Everything that makes me

Speechless.

I am writing to you today,

Marooned in my mind,

Daydreaming on sunny beaches;

With you at my side.

You are the only one

I hope this poem reaches.

Intimacy

Under the cover of night

These sheets are too cold

Without your thighs

Creating friction.

Wonder with all of my might

If secrets should be told

Of what I see in your eyes

When your smile glistens.

You will not lose me tonight

Nor to the elusive mold

Of withering time.

I am yours.

__The Painter__

Some people

Paint with colors

&

Some people

Paint with words.

Heart

Cold hearted individuals,

Praying for a spiritual miracle.

Being heartless gave them strength,

Lovers kept at arms-length.

Heartthrobs cause heartbreaks.

Still,

Heartbeats forever quake..

Quite hearty words

For disheartened nerves;

Maybe I'm just hurt.

<u>Waiting</u>

I found patience

At the edge of my anxieties.

I found patience

Waiting for me

The same way I waited

For something..anything..

And when I finally got there

All was well.

Show Me, Love

Love,

Don't make me

Too blind to see.

Show me

Your flaws

And your

Philosophies.

When Poets Bleed

I bleed like ink from an open book;

I can feel the wound.

Worries sink like stomachs

From an ocean look;

A mind marooned.

I know you bleed the same too;

I'd already assumed.

It's Just A Dream

Life is just a dream

With hopes that it'll be

Just how we dreamt it.

Metaphors do sing.

Like a bird in the sky.

Let me fly

Against the canvas

Generated in my mind.

We are all

The bigger picture

To be identified.

Look within yourself

For the glory.

A Night With Pain

Pain is a funny thing

The way it wants to

Hold hands with us.

It wants to be loved.

It wants to be felt

In the middle of the night.

Pain will give you

Cold embraces

And tell you to

Warm up to it..

But I don't want to

Get used to this.

<u>The End of Us</u>

Don't get jealous,

But I love you even more

In my dreams.

Where everything is lovely

And it's better than it seems..

But my reality is tearing at the seams.

Don't make me have to

Forget you and the beautiful things

I envision when I think about you.

In remembrance of Stace Woodward.

You always told me that I should do something with my poetry, and I always said that I would; but never did..This is my first step in making that happen.

You were a genuine example of living life to the fullest and spreading love and laughter. May your soul be at peace, my friend.

Now that you have taken this journey with me via poetry, I challenge you to try your hand at your own poetry. Use the the free space on pages 13, 17, the next two pages, and the space below to compose your own word art. Write when you are happy, sad, excited, etc. Let it flow and let the ink tell your story:

Social Media Accounts:

Instagram: @_loveislaww
Twitter: @_loveislaw & @zerolaw47

Made in the USA
Middletown, DE
25 April 2021